**Fact Finders**®

## DISCOVER THE NIGHT SKY

# EXPLORING
# AURORAS

BY KAREN LATCHANA KENNEY

Consultant:
Ilia Iankov Roussev, PhD

raintree
a Capstone company — publishers for children

Raintree is an imprint of Capstone Global Library Limited, a company incorporated in England and Wales having its registered office at 264 Banbury Road, Oxford, OX2 7DY – Registered company number: 6695582

www.raintree.co.uk
myorders@raintree.co.uk

Text © Capstone Global Library Limited 2018
The moral rights of the proprietor have been asserted.

ISBN 978 1 4747 4990 9
22 21 20 19 18 17
10 9 8 7 6 5 4 3 2 1

Editorial Credits
Adrian Vigliano, editor; Veronica Scott, designer;
Wanda Winch, media researcher; Gene Bentdahl, production specialist

A full catalogue record for this book is available from the British Library.

Acknowledgements
We would like to thank the following for permission to reproduce photographs: NASA, 21, IMAGE/ UC Berkeley, 26, Johnson Space Center/Earth Science and Remote Sending Unit, 28–29 (background), Polar/University of Iowa, 7, Solar Dynamics Observatory, 14; Newscom: Mondadori Portfolio, 16, Zuma Press/Peter Barritt, 17; Science Source, 11; Shutterstock: Aaron Rutten, 22–23, Atiketta Sangasaeng, 10–11 (background), 27, Georgios Kollidas, 12, MidoSemsem, 8, Mihai Speteanu, 20, muratart, 14–15 (background), Nejron Photo, 24, Nicku, 10, Nicolas Primola, 19, Pavel Vakhrushev, starfield background, Peter Hermes Furian, 13, Phung Chung Chyang, 4–5, 9, Tsuguliev, cover, 25, Zulkefli Mohd Yusop, 18

Printed and bound in China.

THE LONDON BOROUGH
www.bromley.gov.uk

CHISLEHURST
020 8467 1318

Please return/renew this item
by the last date shown.
Books may also be renewed by
phone and Internet.

Bromley Libraries

30128 80316 518 5

# CONTENTS

# CHAPTER 1

# EXPLOSIONS OF LIGHT

On a cold night close to Earth's poles, gaze into the sky. Bright stars twinkle in the dark. Now watch – you are about to see the sky explode with colour. Green light dances above the trees like flames. The light ripples in waves across the sky. Then other colours appear. First you see yellow, then red and even blue. The lights swirl, and the sky shimmers.

What are those lights? This natural light show is an aurora. It can only be seen when it's dark, and only in certain parts of the world. An aurora has different shapes. A curtain shape is thin and flat with folds. An aurora also moves in arcs, bands and patches. An aurora can quickly change shape and colour as it moves.

An aurora shoots upwards through the sky. It is brightest at the bottom and gets fainter the higher up it goes.

## Did you know?

These lights were named after the goddess of dawn from Roman mythology. The goddess Aurora spread the rays of light from the rising Sun.

Auroras happen in two areas on Earth, near the planet's poles. One is in the northern **hemisphere**. The lights here are the **aurora borealis**. Many people call them the northern lights. The best places to see the northern lights are in parts of Canada, Alaska, Iceland and Norway.

Another area is in the southern hemisphere. These lights are the **aurora australis**, also called the southern lights. These lights are harder to see. They happen where few people live, over Antarctica and the southern Indian Ocean.

Auroras happen all year long. You just need a dark and clear sky to see them. Sometimes the lights are dim. At other times, the lights are very bright. You could even read a book by their glow.

An auroral zone is the area where auroras happen. These zones are oval-shaped. They surround Earth's **magnetic poles**.

**hemisphere** – one half of Earth; the equator divides Earth into northern and southern hemispheres

**aurora borealis** – colourful bands of light in the sky of the northern hemisphere, also called the northern lights

**aurora australis** – colourful bands of light in the sky of the southern hemisphere, also called the southern lights

**magnetic pole** – one of two points on Earth's surface where its magnetic pull is the strongest; one is near the geographic North Pole and the other is near the South Pole

# CHAPTER 2

# DISCOVERING AURORAS

People have watched auroras for thousands of years, wondering what they could be. Were they a kind of lightning? Were they spirits in the sky? Were they reflections of the Sun's rays? People wrote about the strange lights in the sky. Some people were frightened by auroras, believing they were signs of bad things to come. Different cultures made up legends to explain what they were.

An early description of auroras was found on a clay tablet from Babylon. The ruins of this ancient city are in modern-day Iraq. The tablet describes a red glow in the night sky in 567 BC. Scientists believe it was an aurora.

Other records tell of these lights too. Ancient Greek thinker Aristotle wrote that the lights came from cracks in the sky. Later records from China and Japan describe red clouds with bands of white. These descriptions might have been referring to the rays of auroras.

Aristotle

# A spirit pathway

One **Inuit** legend explains auroras.
It tells of a lighted pathway in the sky.
Spirits hold torches in a line. The lights
guide new spirits to a hole in the sky.
It leads the spirits to the heavens. The
spirits also feast and play football with
a walrus skull. This makes the lights
dance and move. The spirits try to talk
to people on Earth by making whistles
and cracking sounds. This describes the
sounds people have reported hearing
from auroras.

**Inuit** – people from the Arctic north of Canada, Alaska and Greenland;
they were once known as Eskimos

Scientists began studying auroras. They came up with different theories to try to explain them.

Some thought an aurora was a reflection of moonlight. Italian scientist Galileo Galilei believed water in the air reflected the light. French philosopher René Descartes thought ice crystals did so. Many people believed this theory, but it turned out to be wrong.

Galileo Galilei

Then scientists began to wonder if auroras might be connected to magnetism. It started with British scientist William Gilbert. In the year 1600, he published a book about magnetism. He experimented with magnets and believed Earth was a giant magnet too. It had magnetic poles, just like a magnet.

**William Gilbert**

## Did you know?

Gilbert used a magnet shaped like a **sphere**. He moved a compass around it. The needle always pointed to the north pole of the sphere. This is just how a compass acts on Earth.

**sphere** – round, solid shape such as a ball or globe

British astronomer Edmond Halley was the first to connect auroras with magnetism. He had studied Earth's magnetism for the British navy. Then in 1716 he saw an amazing auroral display. It was the biggest one in a century.

Halley made scientific observations of the event. He saw that the aurora's curtain moved in a certain way. It moved in the direction that a compass needle pointed when hanging in the air. A compass needle always points towards Earth's North Pole. This discovery led Halley to connect the lights with Earth's magnetism.

**Edmond Halley**

He thought matter moved in a **magnetic field** around Earth towards the poles. Then it reacted somehow to make light. It explained why auroras only happen near Earth's poles.

**magnetic field** – area around a magnet that can attract other metals or protect a planet from space particles

# The magnetic Earth

Scientists now know that Gilbert and Halley were right. Earth is a giant magnet. This is because of the planet's layers. At the core is a solid iron ball. Around it is a layer of moving hot liquid metal. Scientists believe that this moving liquid makes the planet magnetic.

A magnetic field flows from the centre of Earth through the South Pole. It moves around the planet and enters at the magnetic North Pole. From there the magnetic field goes back to the centre of Earth again. This forms a giant loop.

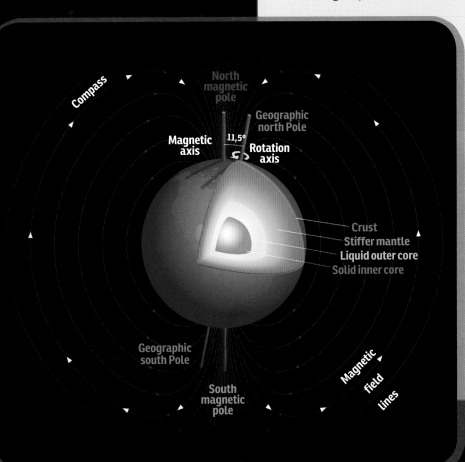

Compass

North magnetic pole

Geographic north Pole

Magnetic axis

11,5°

Rotation axis

Crust
Stiffer mantle
Liquid outer core
Solid inner core

Geographic south Pole

South magnetic pole

Magnetic field lines

Other scientists believed **electricity** in the air caused auroras. Lightning is a form of electricity. It lights up the sky too. Could it be the reason auroras happen?

Benjamin Franklin had experimented with lightning and electricity. He thought lightning might be similar to the northern lights. Franklin wrote a paper about his theory in 1778. He thought electricity moved in warm air. It travelled from tropical areas to the poles. The warm air had so much electricity that it released into the air as light. Other scientists believed in this electricity theory too.

Then on 1 September 1859, British astronomer Richard Carrington saw something strange. He was studying the Sun and noticed bright white light. It erupted from giant spots on the Sun called sunspots. Then it suddenly disappeared. Before dawn the next morning, brilliant auroras lit up skies around Earth. Scientists wondered if the Sun was part of what caused auroras.

Another discovery would help explain an aurora's colours. British scientist Sir William Cooke experimented with gas to see how it glows. He found that moving **electrons** made gas glow. Different types of gases glowed in different colours. And a magnet attracted the glowing light. All of these discoveries added more clues to the mystery of an aurora.

**electricity** – flow or stream of charged particles such as electrons

**electron** – tiny particle with a negative electrical charge that moves around the nucleus of an atom

# CHAPTER 3

# STUDYING THE GLOW

Scientists had found pieces of the puzzle. The Sun seemed to be involved. Earth's magnetism was important. Electricity was part of it too. But how were they all connected?

In the late 1800s, Norwegian physicist Kristian Birkeland made some important connections. He became a pioneer in aurora science. Birkeland watched auroras in northern Norway. He collected data on them. He studied Earth's magnetic field as well. Birkeland also experimented in his laboratory.

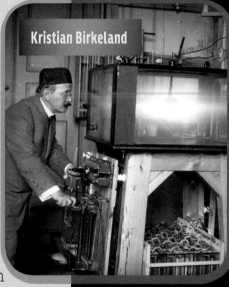

Kristian Birkeland

In 1896 he came up with a theory for what caused an aurora. He believed the Sun was the energy source for auroras. He thought particles from the Sun hit Earth's magnetic field. They moved towards Earth's magnetic poles and hit atoms in the atmosphere. They excited the **atoms** of the **atmosphere**, which caused the glow. Birkeland's theory was partly correct. It greatly advanced our understanding of auroras.

# Polar explorers

The poles were some of the last places on Earth explored by Europeans and Americans. In the late 1800s and early 1900s, expeditions set out to reach the North Pole. Their journeys were long and difficult. They were also filled with amazing views of the northern lights. These explorers later wrote about what they saw. US explorer Frederick Cook wrote a book about his voyage in 1911. He described the aurora as running, liquid fire that glittered in the sky.

Roald Amundsen

Norwegian explorer Roald Amundsen explored the South Pole. He described the aurora as nature wearing its most beautiful dress.

**atom** – smallest part of matter that determines all of its properties

**atmosphere** – gases that surround a planet

Another Norwegian scientist used maths to explain auroras. Carl Störmer was interested in Birkeland's experiments. He thought about Birkeland's theories. Then Störmer discovered how electrons move in the magnetic field using maths.

Störmer began taking photographs of auroras too. In 1909 he set up a system. He found sites in Norway. He connected them by telephone. Several people took photographs of an aurora at the same time. In the two photographs, the aurora appeared in different places.

Störmer used the photographs to measure an aurora's height. He found the bottom of an aurora. He also found the top of an aurora's peaks. He concluded that the lights appear in the ionosphere. This is one of the upper layers of Earth's atmosphere.

ionosphere

Earth's atmosphere has several layers.
People live in the troposphere. Auroras
happen in the ionosphere.

troposphere

Scientists showed that electrons caused an aurora. They seemed to come from the Sun, but how did they cause auroras? In the 1930s British scientist Sydney Chapman came up with a theory. He believed clouds of particles with an electrical charge flowed from the Sun. We now call these clouds **plasma**, a type of matter that exists in space. The plasma flows around Earth's upper atmosphere. Electrical particles in the plasma are part of what causes auroras.

**Van Allen belts**

Then in 1958, US space scientist James Van Allen found another important clue. He was part of a team that launched the first US **satellite** to orbit Earth. The satellite's instruments collected data about the atmosphere. Using the data, Van Allen found electrical particles trapped in the atmosphere. They collected in rings around Earth. Scientists now call these rings the Van Allen belts.

**plasma** – gas containing charged particles
**satellite** – spacecraft that orbits a planet

# CHAPTER 4

# EXPLAINING AURORAS

The first satellites gave us clearer views of space. Since then our technology has improved. Scientists can study our planet, the Sun and space in more advanced ways. Satellites and rockets collect important information. Their images and data have confirmed theories about auroras. We now have proof about why they happen.

An aurora's energy starts at the Sun. The Sun is our star, and it is a burning ball of hydrogen gas. It is the biggest source of energy on Earth and in the solar system. The Sun's atmosphere contains tiny particles. The particles move away from the Sun as gases burn. They move towards Earth in what's called a solar wind. The solar wind is made of plasma.

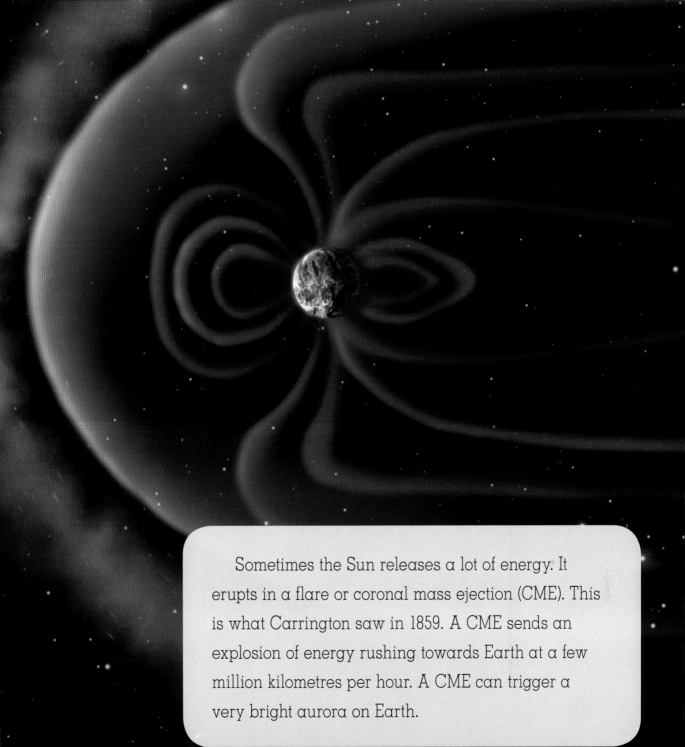

Sometimes the Sun releases a lot of energy. It erupts in a flare or coronal mass ejection (CME). This is what Carrington saw in 1859. A CME sends an explosion of energy rushing towards Earth at a few million kilometres per hour. A CME can trigger a very bright aurora on Earth.

The plasma from the solar wind hits Earth's magnetic field. This field stops many of the Sun's particles from hitting Earth and protects the planet. The Sun's particles also disturb the magnetic field, which contains charged particles. With so much energy, the field becomes unbalanced. It creates an electrical current that releases particles into the atmosphere. The particles rush towards Earth's magnetic poles.

At the poles, the charged particles hit atoms. They transfer the energy to the atoms and excite them. The atoms then release the energy as light.

Different atoms produce different colours. Some oxygen atoms are lower in the atmosphere. This makes a green-yellow aurora. Oxygen atoms higher up make a red aurora. Sometimes an aurora is blue and red near its bottom. This colour comes from hydrogen atoms. Hydrogen and helium atoms can also make a blue-purple aurora.

# Aurora chasers

People are drawn to the colourful beauty of auroras. They are magical sights to see. Some people chase them down every night. These aurora hunters watch weather data. They leave their warm homes on cold nights. They search the sky and hope there are no clouds. With a little luck, they find an aurora. They take stunning photographs and watch the show.

Scientists haven't discovered everything about auroras. They continue to research them. New technology has revealed more about these colourful lights.

Japanese scientist Shun-ichi Akasofu made a discovery using all-sky cameras. These cameras take black and white videos of the entire sky. The videos show an aurora from horizon to horizon. These tools can be used to see the sky from all parts of the world.

Akasofu used data from 100 all-sky cameras. He found that the northern and southern lights were mirror images. They look exactly the same, but are on opposite ends of the planet. Akasofu also found out more about the auroral zone. It is not a perfect oval over the magnetic pole, as scientists previously believed. It is lopsided.

# Aurorasaurus

Anyone can help scientists study auroras. People can use a social media site to report sightings. It's called Aurorasaurus. People send tweets and messages to the site. The reports instantly travel to others around the world, so that people can easily locate an aurora. Scientists still can't predict when an aurora will happen. They can use data from the site to map aurora occurrences. Scientists also hope to use the information to make better forecasts about auroras.

We've learned a lot about auroras from the ground. But the best views come from space. From up there scientists can see an aurora wrap around Earth. Its rays glow, reaching out into space.

Astronauts aboard the International Space Station have the best view. This station orbits Earth. Astronauts live there and observe Earth from space. They take incredible videos and photographs of auroras. Satellites, such as the Suomi-NPP, also record auroras from space. These recordings help scientists to see auroras better. But they do not help scientists learn more about the particles in auroras.

Rockets containing scientific instruments gather information about particles. Scientists shoot rockets through auroras. As the rockets move through them, they collect data about the particles there.

Some mysteries remain about auroras. Scientists still do not know how an aurora's particles move as fast as they do. They also do not know why an aurora forms in thin sheets. Scientists continue to study these glowing lights in the night sky. One day they may find out even more about auroras.

# AURORA TIMELINE:
## FROM SIGHTINGS TO DISCOVERIES

**567 BC**
People from Babylon record an aurora on a clay tablet. It's the first record of an aurora.

**AD 1600**
William Gilbert states that Earth is a magnet.

**1716**
Edmond Halley sees an aurora. He connects it with Earth's magnetism.

**1778**
Benjamin Franklin believes electricity is part of an aurora. Other scientists agree.

**1896**
Kristian Birkeland's theory connects the Sun with auroras.

**1909**
Carl Störmer sets up a system to photograph auroras. He measures the height of an aurora.

**1930s**
Sydney Chapman has a theory about solar wind. It carries electrical particles from the Sun to Earth.

**1958**
James Van Allen discovers rings of electrical particles encircling Earth.

# GLOSSARY

**atmosphere**   gases that surround a planet

**atom**   smallest part of matter that determines all of its properties

**aurora australis**   colourful bands of light in the sky of the southern hemisphere, also called the southern lights

**aurora borealis**   colourful bands of light in the sky of the northern hemisphere, also called the northern lights

**electricity**   flow or stream of charged particles such as electrons

**electron**   tiny particle with a negative electrical charge that moves around the nucleus of an atom

**hemisphere**   one half of Earth; the equator divides Earth into northern and southern hemispheres

**Inuit**   people from the Arctic north of Canada, Alaska and Greenland; they were once known as Eskimos

**magnetic field**   area around a magnet that can attract other metals or protect a planet from space particles

**magnetic pole**   one of two points on Earth's surface where its magnetic pull is the strongest; one is near the geographic North Pole and the other is near the South Pole

**plasma**   gas containing charged particles

**satellite**   spacecraft that orbits a planet

**sphere**   round, solid shape such as a ball or globe

# READ MORE

*Northern Lights* (The Night Sky: and Other Amazing Sights), Nick Hunter (Raintree, 2013)

*The Science Behind Wonders of the Sky* (The Science Behind Natural Phenomena), Allan Morey (Raintree, 2015)

# WEBSITES

**www.dkfindout.com/uk/space/**
Find out more about space!

**www.esa.int/esaKIDSen/**
Learn more from the European Space Agency.

# COMPREHENSION QUESTIONS

1. What happens to give an aurora its colours? What are those colours?

2. How does the timeline show you what scientists have learned about auroras? How is it different from what is explained in the main text?

3. The sidebar entitled "The magnetic Earth" describes why Earth is a magnet. How does this help you to understand more about auroras?

# INDEX